PILGR.

✠

HOLY ISLAND

Also available in the *Pilgrim Guide* series

PILGRIM · GUIDE

HOLY ISLAND

David Adam

Illustrated by
Denise Adam

CANTERBURY
PRESS
Norwich

Text © David Adam 1997
Illustrations © Denise Adam 1997

First published in 1997 by The Canterbury Press Norwich
(a publishing imprint of Hymns Ancient & Modern Limited
a registered charity)
St Mary's Works, St Mary's Plain
Norwich, Norfolk NR3 3BH

British Library Cataloguing in Publication Data

A catalogue record for this book is available
from the British Library

ISBN 1-85311-165-1

Typeset, printed and bound in Great Britain by
The Lavenham Press Ltd,
Lavenham, Suffolk, CO10 9RN

Contents

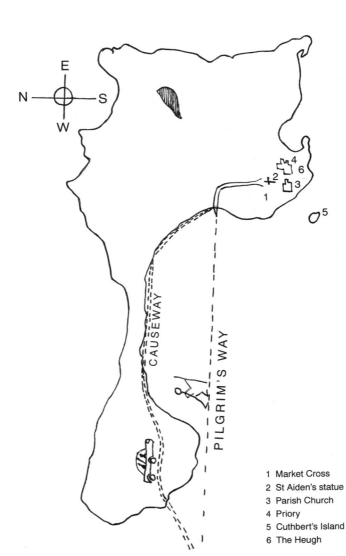

1 Market Cross
2 St Aiden's statue
3 Parish Church
4 Priory
5 Cuthbert's Island
6 The Heugh

vi

1

Introduction:

The Holy Island of Lindisfarne

In the United Kingdom there are at least three islands with the name 'Holy Island'. One is in Wales, at the western tip of Anglesey, where Holyhead, the departure point for ferries to Ireland, is found. Another is in Scotland, in the Firth of Clyde, and is home to a Buddhist monastery. Of the three the Holy Island of Lindisfarne is the best known because of its importance in the history of our land. Time and time again it has been hailed as 'the holiest place in England' on account of the many saints who have lived and worked upon it. The Island is also more accessible than the other two islands bearing the same name as it is only about a mile off the coast of Northumberland and can be approached by road when the tide is out. It can be seen from the A1 road north of Belford, and from the London to Edinburgh railway line. As it is a tidal island, the sea governs the movement of the fishermen, the lugworm diggers, the day visitors, the pilgrims, the residents, and the thousands of birds along the shoreline.

The first mention we have of Holy Island in literature is in the 570s at the death of Urien-ap-Rheged, a Christian king who was trying to drive the pagan English out of Bernicia, which stretched north of the River Tees up to what is now East Lothian. The Island was then known as 'Inis Metcaut'. The writer Taliesin tells how Urien and his men besieged the Island for three days and three nights. Taliesin calls Urien 'king of the baptized world'; he also tells how Urien was a cattle rustler! Urien was betrayed by some of his own company and beheaded. This was a decisive battle for it was the last great stand of the British against the incoming English in the north of England. The early Irish monks also

1

knew the Island by its Celtic name of Inis Metcaut, but it soon took on the name of Lindisfarne when Aidan set up his monastery and mission station there.

Writing from the court of Charlemagne, after the Viking invasion in 793, Alcuin describes the Island as 'a place more venerable than all in Britain'. This was because from the seventh century it had become a great place of pilgrimage. It was certainly the most popular shrine in the north, if not in all of England. Here people came for hope and for healing, for peace and for direction. Many came especially because the incorrupt body of Cuthbert was in the Church of St Peter. This would have continued if it were not for the Viking invasions. It would seem that these, and the monks' removal of many of the saints' bones, including the incorrupt body of Cuthbert, brought a great diminishment in the number of pilgrims. The Island would have had very few people, if any, left on it by the time Cuthbert's relics were removed. After the Viking invasion we know very little about the island until the coming of the Benedictine monks.

It was the Benedictine monks, coming from Durham in the twelfth century, who called the island 'Holy Island'. Holy Island is the popular name, used by the islanders and most of the people of Northumberland. Some call it 'The Holy Island of Lindisfarne'. It is said that it was called 'Holy Island' in memory of all the saints who gave their lives here, especially those who died at the hands of the Vikings.

Now there are some places that keep a feeling of the past; Holy Island is one of them. In a television series about 'Holy England' it was said: 'Of all of Holy England, Holy Island is the holiest of all.' There is a feel about the Island, especially when the tide is in, that it is different, a place set apart and one which invites us to set ourselves apart. It invites us to experience its vast expanses of sea and sky, and great sweeps of the mainland of England and Scotland. It invites us to walk where the saints have walked, and to pray where they

have prayed. It invites us to expand our vision. It invites us
to be pilgrims.

The Invitation

God calls you out from where you are.
God calls you from your safety and security.
Come!
Come to the Borderlands where sea meets sky.
Come to the edge where earth meets sea.
Come!
Come where two worlds meet.
Come and discover that heaven and earth are one.
Come!
You are children of the way,
You have a road to travel.
Come!
You need a Holy Island,
A holy place that makes all places holy.
Come!
You have a rendezvous to make,
A meeting place to find.
Come!
Listen to the waves and the murmur of God.
Be moved by the wind, and the calling of God.
Come!
Let walking become your prayer,
Let journeying be part of your song.
Come!
You may discover yourself,
You may meet your own mysterious being.
Come!
Discover for yourself sacred space.
Enter into the time which is beyond time.
Come!

Then everywhere will be changed,
Every place will be transformed.
Come!
It is God who calls you to step out,
It is God who travels the road with you.
Come!

As you set out on your pilgrimage you might like to use a prayer by Alcuin, who said that Holy Island was the holiest place in England:

Eternal Light, shine in our hearts;
Eternal Goodness, deliver us from evil,
Eternal Power, be our support;
Eternal Wisdom, scatter the darkness of our ignorance;
Eternal Pity, have mercy upon us;
that with all our heart and mind and strength we may seek your face
and be brought, by your infinite mercy, to your holy presence;
through Jesus Christ our Lord.

2

The Pilgrim's Way

For over 1300 years pilgrims have made their way to the Holy Island of Lindisfarne, to see where the saints lived and to be near where they were buried. Both Aidan and Cuthbert were originally buried on the Island. From the seventh century people flocked to the shrine seeking healing and peace. Because of quicksands, and the twisting journey of the River Low, the Pilgrim's Way had to be clearly marked out. First there were cairns, little piles of stones, put up by the monks to guide the travellers. Posts were put in the sands in 1860 as a clear guide to islanders and travellers. Still too many lives were being lost to the tide: the Parish Registers regularly note persons being drowned. A new set of poles was erected in 1987, commemorating the 1300 years since Cuthbert's death.

The roadway, though begun in 1954, was really completed in 1965 when the part crossing the River Low was raised above the level of the sands and provided with a

refuge box for tide-stranded travellers. At all times it must be remembered that the Pilgrim's Way and the metalled causeway are part of the tidal flats. Every day, twice in twenty-four hours, the tide will come in, covering the sands and cutting the Island off. No journey should be attempted without first checking on the tides, and remembering the tide comes in quicker on the Pilgrim's Way than on the modern road. Large pilgrim groups need to be particularly careful, and it is not a good idea to walk the roadway, for it is too busy. It cannot be emphasized enough that this is the sea you are dealing with. A few extracts from the Parish Registers might help to remind you:

Jan. 8th 1584, old John Stapleton drowned
Nov. 5th 1641 Samuel Waddell and his son drowned in the Low
July 28th 1746 Rob Brown, Clerk of Holy Island drowned
April 8th 1801 William Macmillan drowned in passing the sands
Dec. 15th 1802 Alexander Warwick drowned in crossing the sands

Do take care; there is no danger at all if you follow the tide tables. These can be found at the turn-off from the A1, at the beginning of the causeway, and on the Island. Information concerning the tides can be had from the Tourist Board in Berwick-upon-Tweed.

The Venerable Bede describes the Island and its tides:

As the tide ebbs and flows, this place is surrounded twice daily by the waves of the sea like an island, and twice, when the sands are dry, it becomes again attached to the mainland.[1]

Sir Walter Scott, in the epic poem *Marmion*, captures the scene romantically:

The tide did now its flood-mark gain,
And girdled in the Saint's domain:
For, with the flow and ebb its style
Varies from continent to isle;
Dry shod o'er sands, twice every day,
The pilgrims to the shrine find way;
Twice every day, the waves efface
Of staves and sandall'd feet the trace.

[*Marmion* 2. 8]

The journey across the sands is very much like our journey through life, or our approach to prayer. Sometimes the way is clear and the passage is easy. At other times the way ahead is closed and we can do nothing about it. No amount of jumping up and down will change it, all we can do is quietly wait. There are times when we must move forward without delay or it will be too late. Sometimes we are all at sea and at other times the road is wide open for us to travel it. At all times we need to accept the guidance of those who have gone before us and heed what they say. We need to plan our journey carefully and be aware of the hazards that can meet us.

We all need to seek our own Holy Island, a place that is sometimes set apart and cut off. If we do not have a Holy Island we need to create one. We need to be able to carry a Holy Island in our heart. Place is important and we all need a holy place, a sacred place, a place where we meet with the Holy One. It is important that Pilgrims take this holy place with them wherever they travel. We are travelling in depth as well as laterally; this is what distinguishes us from tourists. We are on an inward journey as well as one over the countryside. A saying I like which applies to pilgrimage is: 'Traveller, there is no road, the road is made as you go.' A comment by St Augustine of Hippo is a worthy thought for our journey:

People travel to wonder
at the height of the mountains,
at the huge waves of the sea,
at the long courses of rivers,
at the vast compass of the ocean,
at the circular motion of the stars,
and pass by themselves without wondering.[2]

On the Pilgrim's Way there are two refuge boxes just in case you have tried to beat the tide! Stop at one of these and think. There are times in life when we cannot save ourselves. We have suddenly come up against a power that is stronger than we are. Suddenly we can find ourselves in deep water. We may know where we should be, but now there will be no achieving it without help. Sometimes the wisdom of the past comes to our rescue, the care of those who have gone before us provides us with help. At other times help is forthcoming from the vigilance of the people of today.

If you are truly stuck in a refuge box on the causeway, you may be rescued by the North Sunderland lifeboat, or a Sea King helicopter from RAF Boulmer. There is never need for this if you plan your journey. Allow an hour and a half to walk the sands from the point where you are over the River Low until you reach the village. Begin your journey across the sands with prayer and praise:

God bless us on our pilgrimage,
Your Presence guide our journey:
Your strength support us in our travels:
Your peace be on the road we take:
Grant us a vision of your kingdom:
Give us a glimpse of your glory:
Bless us in our pilgrimage.

Here is a suggested *Benedicite* for your walking; do add verses of your own devising:

O all you powers of the Lord,
Bless you the Lord, praise and magnify Him forever.

O all you pilgrims of God,
O all you servants of Christ,
O all you people of the Spirit,
Bless you the Lord, praise and magnify Him forever.

O all you saints of Holy Island,
O Aidan, Colman and Cuthbert,
O all you abbots and priors,
Bless you the Lord, praise and magnify Him forever.

O all you missionaries from Holy Island,
O Chad, Cedd and Wilfrid,
O you mighty preachers,
Bless you the Lord, praise and magnify Him forever.

O all you birds of the sands,
O curlew, sanderling and godwit,
O plover, turnstone and sandpiper,
Bless you the Lord, praise and magnify Him forever.

O you birds of the waters,
O eider duck, shelduck and cormorant,
O shag, oystercatcher and fulmar,
Bless you the Lord, praise and magnify Him forever.

O you creatures of the shoreline,
O you crab, winkle and lugworm,
O you sea pinks, campion and bladderwrack,
Bless you the Lord, praise and magnify Him forever.

O all you who journey today,
O all you pilgrims and seekers,
O all you tourists and travellers,
Bless you the Lord, praise and magnify Him forever.

3

The Market Cross

When you have crossed the sands follow the metalled road into the village. At the crossroads go straight over and head for the market place. The main street which you have crossed is Marygate and you are walking down Crossgates. The links with the past are shown in the street and place names: Minster Close, Sanctuary Close, Easter Field, Palace Hill, Cuddy (St Cuthbert's) Walls, Prior Lane, Popple Well, Baggot (Backgate), Tripping Chare, Cuthbert's Square, Fiddler's Green, Fenkle (Crooked) Street.

Holy Island village is referred to by the locals as 'the town'. It was in the late Middle Ages that Holy Island, small as it is, was made a town. As a town it had its own market day on a Saturday. There might have been an idea of making the Island into a larger township, but the regular warfare with Scotland and the awkwardness of the tide prevented this ever happening.

Here in the centre of the village is the Market Cross. The upper part of the cross has been replaced in the 1990s after a great gale blew the top off and it broke into pieces. An even earlier top to the cross can be seen in the Priory museum. We know that in 1825 only the socket of the cross remained and that a Mr H. C. Selby had a new cross erected, which was no doubt a copy of the old one. This cross cost £100.

Here at the centre of the village, where notices would be given out, where commerce went on and pilgrims went to and fro, stands the cross. Here where singers perform, bands play and Morris Men dance, is the cross. As in many villages up and down the country the cross has been given central place because it affects all of life. As you would expect on Holy Island it is a traditional Celtic cross, a circle on which the cross is laid. The image is the circle of the world made

one in the Cross of Christ. The cross is not just for the church but for the whole world, so it is set up in the Market Place. The cross affects not only what we do in church, not only our own lives, but the whole of creation. Through the Cross of Christ the world is made whole. Listen again to words from Alcuin:

We should glory in the Cross of Christ for he is our salvation.
He is our life, He is the hope of our resurrection.
Through Him we are made whole and set free.
We should glory in the Cross of Christ.
Adore the lifted standard of the Cross, O faithful soul.
Who takes it for his sign, need fear no sorrow.
That blessed Cross, where the Lord's body hung,
And by His dying closed the road to death.
He that created life, slew death by dying.
And by His wounds the world's wounds are made whole.

On the statue of Aidan, which we shall go to next, is a similar Celtic cross. There is a further Celtic cross head, perhaps the old Market Cross, in the English Heritage museum at the Priory. There are the bases of two other large standing crosses on the Island. The first, near the east end of the church and the west door of the Priory, is called 'The Petting Stone'. This is the base of a very large cross. It is the custom for brides, supported by two fishermen, to jump over this base immediately after their wedding in church for good luck. There is a further base of a high cross of later date in the Priory Church against the northern wall. The modern war memorial cross on the 'Heugh' was designed by Lutyens, and there is the possibility of another cross base on the Heugh, south of the war memorial.

At the centre of the village let us give thanks for the history of the Island and pray for the people who live here and visit here today. Give thanks that the Cross has had central place, and pray it may continue to do so. The following prayer is attributed to St Aidan and is used daily on the Island at Marygate House, which is an ecumenical Retreat House. Here in the centre of the 'town' pray for its people:

Lord, this bare island,
Make it your place of peace.
Here be the peace of men who do your will:
Here be the peace of brothers serving men:
Here be the peace of holy rules obeying:
Here be the peace of praise by dark and day.
Be this your island, your holy island.
Lord, your servants speak this prayer.
Be it your care. Amen.

And before leaving the Market Place a prayer to the Christ of the Cross, 'that by his wounds the wounds of the world are made whole':

Christ broken for us on the cross,
We come to you, for you alone can make us whole.

We come with the broken hearted and broken spirited,
We come with the broken in mind, the broken in body.
We come to you, for you alone can make us whole.

We come with those of broken relationships and broken homes,
We come with those of broken promises and broken dreams.
We come to you, for you alone can make us whole.

We come with broken hopes and broken trusts,
We come as broken people in a broken world.
We come to you, for you alone can make us whole.

We come on our pilgrimage for wholeness, health and healing,
We come for unity, harmony and peace.
We know that you Christ of the cross can make us whole.
Alleluia. Amen.

4

St Aidan's Statue

We go past the Priory museum into the churchyard and to the statue of St Aidan. The view of the Castle with this statue has become one of the great symbols of Northumberland. The statue was created by Miss Kathleen Parbury and placed here for the visit of Her Majesty the Queen in 1958. The statue is eleven feet high. Aidan holds in one hand a crozier, as a sign that he is a bishop: in the other hand he holds his torch of flame, and he looks southwards towards what would be his main mission field.

After the battle of Heavenfield in 634, King Oswald of Northumbria invited the monks of Iona to send some of their members to be missionaries in Northumbria. Abbot Segene sent Corman but he found that he could make no headway with the Angles of Northumbria and soon returned to Iona. There was danger that the mission would be seen as a failure. When Corman arrived back at Iona they had a meeting about his return, at which Aidan stood up and said: 'It seems to me, brother, that you were too hard on your ignorant hearers. You should have followed the practice of the Apostles, and begun by giving them the milk of simpler teaching until little by little, as they were nourished on the Word of God, they grew capable of greater understanding.'

By such words Aidan virtually volunteered to replace Corman and was sent to Northumbria. It is believed he brought another twelve monks with him, as was the Celtic tradition. In looking for a site for his monastic settlement Aidan chose the island of Inis Metcaut, as it was close to the capital at Bamburgh and yet cut off enough for them to develop their lifestyle of prayer and devotion. Aidan knew they needed to be near the capital to reach out to the English, but if they were too close it would alienate them from the indigenous British who also needed pastoral care. Many of the British would be lapsed Christians who had been persecuted by the incoming English. Much of this mission would need to be one of reconciliation.

Very soon school, mission station and church were all in action; there was also a scriptorium for producing books. In the school members of the royal court and freed slaves would be offered the same education. One of the aims of the school was to provide, as soon as possible, indigenous priests to further the gospel in the land. Aidan understood that to make mission last it had to be local, and led by local people.

Aidan chose to walk, whenever it was practical, so that he could meet people and talk to them. He simply asked if they were Christian. If they were he would encourage them to pray and would pray with them; if they were not he would ask, 'Why not?' Bede says of him:

> He gave his clergy an inspiring example of self-discipline and continence, and the highest recommendation of his teaching to all was that he and his followers lived as they taught. He never sought or cared for any worldly possessions, and loved to give away to the poor whatever he received from kings or wealthy folk. Whether in town or country, he always travelled on foot, unless compelled by necessity to ride, and whenever he met anyone, high or low he stopped and spoke to them. If they were heathen, he urged them to be baptised: and if they were Christians, he strengthened their faith, and inspired them by word and deed to live a good life and to be generous to others. [3]

Bede continues:

> He cultivated peace and love, purity and humility: he was above anger and greed, despised pride and conceit; he set himself to keep and teach the laws of God, and was diligent in study and

in prayer. He used his priestly authority to check the proud and the powerful: he tenderly comforted the sick; he relieved and protected the poor. ... I greatly admire and love all these things about Aidan, because I have not doubt that they are pleasing to God. [4]

It is not surprising that Bede says of him, 'His life is in marked contrast to the apathy of our times.' Any who look at the life of Aidan cannot but be moved and challenged. Such a life bore much fruit. The mission flourished and children were sent to the school to be taught. From one family came four brothers, of whom all would become priests and two would be bishops: they were Cedd, Caelin, Cynebil and Chad. Cedd founded churches as far away as Essex, of which St Peter's at Bradwell-on-Sea still stands; he also founded a church and monastery at Lastingham in North Yorkshire. Chad was the first bishop of Mercia and Lindsey at Lichfield. Like his teacher, Chad preferred to walk rather than ride so that he could meet people on their level. Another student, Wilfrid, founded the Abbey at Hexham and was responsible for the building of a great church at Ripon. The crypts of these churches survive. Wilfrid was also responsible for extensive missionary work among the south Saxons in what is now Sussex. Abroad he worked in what is now Holland and Belgium winning souls for Christ. Aidan also persuaded St Hilda not to leave for a monastery in France and saw that she was given land for a foundation in Northumbria. Later she would be the Abbess of the great monastery at Whitby.

For sixteen years Aidan was bishop of Lindisfarne. It is interesting to think how those years spent here at Lindisfarne have influenced the whole history of our land. There is no doubt that it was Aidan's holiness that attracted Cuthbert and made him offer himself at Melrose. From this little Island the light shone out in what are known as the 'Dark

Ages'. Though Aidan bore the torch, that light was the Light of Christ. It was because of the great missionary thrust begun by Aidan that Bishop Lightfoot of Durham said, 'Augustine was the apostle of Kent, but Aidan was the apostle of England.'

Let us give thanks for the founder of the church on this island, for his example, and for his great missionary outreach, and let us dedicate ourselves to the service of God:

For all who have handed on your light;
We thank you, Holy Lord.
For all who have proclaimed your presence;
We thank you, Holy Lord.
For all who have taught of your love;
We thank you, Holy Lord.
For all who have set the captives free;
We thank you, Holy Lord.
For all who inspired us by their example;
We thank you, Holy Lord.
For all who have left us a great heritage;
We thank you, Holy Lord.
For Aidan and the saints of this Holy Island;
We thank you, Holy Lord.

Lord, open our eyes to your glory,
Open our ears to your call,
Open our hearts to your love,
Open our lives to your presence,
Guide us on our pilgrimage through life,
That with the love of Aidan in our hearts,
The inspiration of Aidan in our minds,
We may dedicate ourselves to you,
And find our freedom in your service,
Through Jesus Christ our Lord.

5

The Parish Church

At one time there were four or five churches on the island –
the Parish Church, the Priory Church, St Cuthbert's by the
Sea on St Cuthbert's Island, and a church out at St Coombs
Farm dedicated to St Columba; there was probably also a
little church on the hill called the Heugh. The Priory stands
immediately to the east of the Parish Church on almost the
same alignment and axis. It is not unusual for important
early church sites to have one church for conventual use and
another as the parish church. Bede says that Bishop Finan
built 'a church suitable for an episcopal see', and that it was
dedicated to St Peter by Archbishop Theodore. Aidan's
body, which had been in the monastic cemetery, was translated into this 'greater church' and placed on the right side
of the altar. In 687 Cuthbert's body was buried in St Peter's

at the right side of the altar, and was raised up on the same spot eleven years later. The phrase 'greater church' can well mean 'the greater of the two', and the Parish Church would be the lesser of the two.

In the ninth century Bishop Ecgred moved a church, which had been built by Aidan in the time of Oswald, from Lindisfarne to Norham and rebuilt it there. Since this church was portable it must have been timber built and could hardly have been described as 'a church suitable for an episcopal see'. Its survival for almost two hundred years suggests that it had been deliberately preserved as a relic or shrine, perhaps in a later stone building. Since most of the early Minsters in the seventh and eighth centuries were dedicated to the Virgin, the dedication of the Parish Church to 'St Mary the Virgin' also hints that it could be earlier than St Peter's. It could well be that the Parish Church is on the site of Aidan's church and the Priory on the site of St Peter's where Aidan and Cuthbert were buried.

A story told by Reginald of Durham during the episcopate of Hugh du Puiset (1153–95) describes a miraculous appearance of Cuthbert. Those who witnessed it saw Cuthbert and his followers coming out of the Parish Church and going to the Priory by the west door, they celebrated mass in the Priory and then returned to St Mary's. Certainly both churches were in existence then and, it would seem, both in use.

The present Parish Church is now the oldest building on the Island, and the only one that now has any Saxon work within it. In the wall that divides the nave from the chancel is a little Saxon arch, touching the later Early English arch. High above this is a typical Saxon 'door'. On the outside of the building, looking from the Priory towards the church, where the nave joins the chancel, you can see Saxon quoin stones, some of them now very worn. We shall never know for sure, but some of these Saxon stones might just be the ones that surrounded Aidan's wooden church. It could very well be that Aidan worshipped here and that there has been a church on this site since 635.

There is no doubt that the Norman work in the twelfth century was not a building but an extending or re-ordering of a building, just as the Early English work was about a hundred years later. It would seem that the church was extended at about the time the Priory was built. This gave the church its three rounded Norman arches on the north side. The alternating of red and white stone in these arches is the only example to be found in Northumberland. When the Priory Church got its Early English extension, then the Parish Church got its southern arches and aisle. These are the pointed arches which include a small one to the back of the north side of the church and the chancel arch. The chancel is also Early English, with three beautiful long lancet windows in the east. When the Priory got its enlarged chancel, it would seem the Parish Church was given one also. The main shape of the church as we see it today was completed in the thirteenth century. It is likely that the Benedictine monks used the Parish Church until the Priory Church was completed.

There are various memorials in the church, the oldest of which is inset into the north wall of the chancel and appears to be a mitre and a cross, with a sword. This is likely to be from the twelfth century. Under the chancel arch on the south side is a memorial to Sir William Reed of Fenham who died in 1604. On it is the inscription *Contra vim mortis non est medicamen in hortis*, which translates as 'Against the power of death there is no remedy in the garden'. In the sanctuary the reredos has St Aidan, St Cuthbert, Bede, Oswald, Columba and Wilfrid, as well as the blessed Virgin and St John at the foot of the cross: a reminder that we are surrounded by the whole company of heaven.

In front of the altar is a beautiful Celtic carpet. This is a copy of the St Mark 'carpet page' of the Lindisfarne Gospels, and was thus designed by Eadfrith, Bishop of Lindisfarne. It is fitting that a page from the Lindisfarne Gospels should find its way into a carpet in the place where Eadfrith lived and worked. This carpet was the idea of Miss Kathleen Parbury, who directed the work on it. Students from Alnwick College of Education transferred the design onto canvas, and the carpet was then made by eighteen women from the Island.

It is worth looking at the list of saints on the west wall of the church and giving thanks for what they have left for us – not only those on the board but all the unknown worshippers who have helped to make this such a holy place. Prayer has been offered here for over 1300 years. Do not leave without adding a prayer to all those that have gone before. Think upon these words:

> *Give thanks to the Father who has delivered us from the dominion of darkness and made us partakers of the inheritance of His saints in light.*

Quietly, in this church, give thanks for Aidan and Cuthbert, for the light that shone out in the Dark Ages, for all who have worshipped here and for the pilgrims of today. You may like to look at the Aidan window at the west end of the church. See how the Island runs through his heart. See how his torch burns brightly. Pray for the Island and its ministry:

We remember before you, O Lord,
All who come on pilgrimage and all who worship here.
Lord hear our prayer.
We remember all who seek your presence,
Lord hear our prayer.
We remember all who heed your call,
Lord hear our prayer.
We remember all who long for you,
Lord hear our prayer.
We remember all who are testing their vocations,
Lord hear our prayer.
We remember that you have called us here,
Lord hear our prayer.

Bless, O Lord, this Island, this Holy Island,
Make it a place of peace and love,
Make it a place of joy and light,
Make it a place of holiness and hospitality,
Make it a place of grace and goodness,
And begin with me.

6

St Cuthbert

There is a Cuthbert window on the north side of the west wall of the church. There is also a painted replica of his coffin, an icon, and a painting of the departure of the monks with his incorrupt body from the Island.

It was on 31st August 651, when St Aidan died, that Cuthbert had his vision and call. Bede says:

> *On a certain night while his companions were sleeping, he himself was keeping watch and praying according to his custom, when he suddenly saw a stream of light from the sky breaking in upon the darkness of the long night. In the midst of this, the choir of the heavenly hosts descending to the earth, and taking with them, without delay, a soul of exceeding brightness, returned to their heavenly home.*[5]

Cuthbert discovered the next day that Aidan had died, so he went to offer himself at the monastery at Melrose.

After training at Melrose Cuthbert went to Ripon to help found a monastery there. At Ripon Cuthbert was the guest-master. It was here that he met with an angelic visitor in the guise of a poor man seeking food and shelter. Bede writes of Cuthbert and his caring for others:

> *Above all else he was afire with heavenly love, unassumingly patient, devoted to unceasing prayer, and kindly to all who came to him for comfort. He regarded the labour of helping the weaker brethren with advice as equivalent to prayer, remembering that He who said 'Thou shalt love the Lord thy God' also said 'love thy neighbour'.*[6]

From Ripon Cuthbert returned to Melrose and here, with the Prior Boisil and many others, he caught the Yellow Plague. In the last days of Boisil's life, Cuthbert meditated with him on St John's Gospel. Cuthbert recovered from the plague to continue his life of dedication. He was made the Prior of Melrose in about 661. Immediately, Cuthbert showed great concern for the people of the area, for the poor and the ill. The plague was still rife and people were losing faith. He went deep into the hill country in his concern for those in remote areas. He was sometimes away from Melrose for a whole month, teaching and caring for the sick, strengthening people in their faith as well as in their bodies.

While Prior of Melrose he visited the monastery at Coldingham, high on the cliffs facing the North Sea. The abbess in charge of this monastery of men and women was Ebba, sister of King Oswald. Cuthbert left the monastery at night for the lonely shore. He walked into the sea and spent the night there in vigil, with his arms outstretched in the form of the cross. At dawn Cuthbert came out from the sea and there immediately followed him two otters. These creatures rubbed themselves against his feet and did not leave until he blessed them. A brother from Coldingham was spying on him and related this story.

After the Synod of Whitby in 664, Cuthbert, then about thirty years old, became the Prior of Lindisfarne. It was his task to bring the brothers that had not left for Iona and Ireland to the usage of the Roman Catholic Church. This cannot have been easy for him but by example and patience he won the day. There is no doubt that his own devotion and dedication would be an inspiration to the brethren.

Whilst he was Prior on Lindisfarne Cuthbert's fame spread as a healer and a spiritual counsellor, and people flocked to come and see him. While looking after the Island he was so occupied that he often went three or four nights without sleep. During this time he would recite psalms whilst doing some manual work or walking around the Island and seeing how all was getting on; sometimes he would go off to the little island next to his monastery.

Life on the Island was obviously very demanding and full of people. Even on the little island next to the monastery Cuthbert's prayer time was being invaded. He needed more time in solitude, to be alone with God. In 676 he ceased being Prior and withdrew to the island of Inner Farne, where Aidan had spent some time before him. He obtained permission from his friend, the abbot Eata, to seek a place for solitude and unbroken prayer. He was then in his early forties. Bede writes:

> *He joyfully entered into the remote solitudes which he had long desired, sought and prayed for, with the good will of that same abbot and also the brethren. He rejoiced because, after a long and blameless active life, he was now counted worthy to rise to the repose of divine contemplation.*[7]

Cuthbert, very like tidal Holy Island, recognized the need for rhythm in life. It cannot all be open – or all closed – life needs a balance. Sometimes we need to be very much part of the mainland and all that is going on; at other times we need to separate out and be an island for a while. We all need space, a time set apart, free from noise and busyness. If we cannot find an island we need to create one. Perpetual busyness is a great danger to the life of the spirit.

On Inner Farne there is a story about Cuthbert dealing with birds that were stealing thatch from the roof of his house. He spoke to them; and the birds, being reprimanded, left. This made Cuthbert feel guilty, and he prayed for their return. When they came back they brought a large piece of fat which Cuthbert accepted as a gift, using it to waterproof his boots. It must have been at this time that he developed his love for the eider duck, which in Northumberland is affectionately called 'Cuddy's Duck'.

Here he built his hermitage and a place for guests.

Though far more difficult to reach, Inner Farne is still only a mile off the coast and people still came in great numbers to see Cuthbert. He even had a guest house built. He planned to spend the rest of his life on Inner Farne, but the church in its wisdom thought differently. In 684 he was elected by Archbishop Theodore and King Egfrith as the Bishop of Hexham. On Easter Day 685 Cuthbert was consecrated Bishop at York by Archbishop Theodore. Almost immediately he exchanged the see of Hexham with Eata, and Cuthbert became the Bishop of Lindisfarne. It was for slightly less than two years that Cuthbert was a bishop. He returned in ailing health to Lindisfarne and then to his hermitage on Inner Farne.

Cuthbert died on Inner Farne on 20th March 687. His body was brought over the water by the monks and was buried at Lindisfarne. Already it was felt that they had the remains of an important saint, just what the north needed. Eleven years later when his body was dug up so that the remains might be elevated – this was the way of declaring him a saint – the incorruption of his body was discovered. From that time onwards pilgrims flocked to the Island to be near this holy man in this holy place and to see this miracle.

Because of the many pilgrims that came bearing gifts the shrine became rich indeed, far removed from what it was like in the days of Aidan. It is just possible that the first Vikings to invade, in 793, had done their homework beforehand and knew that here were great treasures and only monks to defend them. It would be far easier to attack Lindisfarne than a fortress like Bamburgh. The invasion of Lindisfarne sent shockwaves around Europe, not only because the holy place was attacked but because the invasions by such boats changed the feeling of safety anywhere in Britain and in much of Europe. On the Island, monks were killed or taken as slaves, and some were driven into the sea to drown.

The treasures of the shrine were taken. But for some strange reason Cuthbert, the Lindisfarne Gospels, and many relics were left untouched. After a while the monastery and shrine were both in use once more.

In 875, however, when the Vikings raided Tynemouth Priory and destroyed it, Bishop Eardulph of Lindisfarne decided it was time for the monks to leave the Island and take with them the relics of Cuthbert. This group, known as 'The Cuthbert Congregation', travelled around northern England and the south-west corner of Scotland seeking a safe home for the body of Cuthbert and other relics. For a while they rested at Norham on the banks of the Tweed, then moved around the borders before going southwards. They settled at Chester-le-Street in County Durham for over a hundred years. Yet another Danish scare forced them to move. They reached as far as Ripon in north Yorkshire and then turned back northwards. Finally, in 995, they came to Durham. A Saxon church was built and Cuthbert's relics were translated to it in 999.

Under Bishop William of Calais, Durham became a Benedictine monastic see in 1083. In 1104 Cuthbert's body was once again examined and found incorrupt, and then placed in the new Norman cathedral.

In 1828 the secondary relics, such as the pectoral cross,

St Cuthbert's cross

stole and vestments, and the wooden coffin, were removed from the tomb and can now all be seen on display at the cathedral. The Lindisfarne Gospels and the uncial Gospel of St John are in the British Library.

Give thanks for all who have come to this Island and found healing and hope, peace and purpose, and for all who have been inspired to go from here and do new things for God. Look at the Cuthbert window, notice the cross and the terns, and give thanks for the beauties of creation and for the ministry of St Cuthbert:

For the rising and the setting sun,
Glory and praise to you, O God.
For the multitude of islands and continents,
Glory and praise to you, O God.
For the varieties of peoples and their gifts,
For the wonders of creation and the mystery of life,
Glory and praise to you, O God.
For all creatures upon earth, for all living things,
Glory and praise to you, O God.
For sea and sky and air, for the glories of the landscape,
Glory and praise to you, O God.

Father, we give you thanks that you called Cuthbert from the tending of sheep to be a shepherd of your flock. We give thanks for all who have been faithful shepherds in this place, the saints, the bishops, priors, vicars and all who have ministered here throughout the ages. We join our prayers with the prayers of all who have gone before us. We pray for the ministry of your church, for its preaching and healing ministry and for our share in that ministry. By the inspiration of Cuthbert make us faithful, patient, and prayerful. We ask this in the name of Christ our living Lord.

7

The Lindisfarne Gospels

The Lindisfarne Gospels were created 'for God and for Saint Cuthbert, and, jointly, for the saints whose relics are on this island'. The Gospels were specially prepared for the time when St Cuthbert's body would be elevated – that is, eleven years after his death. So it is likely that they were completed by the year 698. It would seem that the special coffin to contain the elevated bones of the saint was prepared at the same time.

The Lindisfarne Gospels are made up of the four Gospels and have 516 pages: this would take at least 129 hides of calf skin to make. Each skin measured slightly more than two feet wide and was about fifteen inches in depth. Examination of the pages has revealed that the spines of the animals ran horizontally across the pages. Every four skins are made into a gathering of sixteen pages.

To produce the Gospels another copy would have had to be at hand for the two years that it took to produce this wonderful work. The copy used was the Vulgate of St Jerome, and the dedication in the Lindisfarne Gospels links this book with Naples. It is thought that this copy might have been borrowed from the monastery at Jarrow. There is an Anglo-Saxon riddle which describes the making of a book, from getting the skin until the actual binding and decorating of the book:

*An enemy ended my life, deprived me of my physical strength:
then he dipped me in water and drew me out again, and put me
in the sun, where I soon shed all my hair. After that, the knife's
sharp edge bit into me and all my blemishes were scraped away;
fingers folded me, and a bird's feather often moved over my
brown surface, sprinkling meaningful marks: it swallowed*

*more wood dye and again travelled over me leaving black
tracks. Then a man bound me, he stretched skin over me and
adorned me with gold; thus I am enriched by the wondrous work
of smiths, wound about with shining metal.*[8]

The scribe chose to use as his lettering the formal script
known as 'Insular Majuscule Script' which originated in Ireland and became a speciality of the British Isles. This made a
rather fine book, not meant for the library but for ceremonial
use within the church, and even then perhaps only on very
special festivals.

Fifteen of the pages are elaborately decorated. Each
Gospel has a page showing the Evangelist and his symbols,
a 'carpet page' of intricate interweaving based around a
cross, and a major initial page. St Matthew has a second initial page at Chapter one, verse eighteen, to mark the story of
the Incarnation. At the beginning of the Gospels there is St
Jerome's letter to Pope Damascus: this has an initial and a
carpet page. Before the Gospels, in one gathering of sixteen
pages, are decorated arcades containing the Eusebian canon
tables. These are tables devised early in the fourth century
by Eusebius, Bishop of Caesarea, to provide a system of
easily locating parallel passages in the four Gospels. One of
the most famous pages is the beginning of St Luke's Gospel
where the artist has used over ten thousand red dots to make
a pattern. On the St Mark's carpet page it has been calculated
that there are more than seven thousand intersections without one mistake.

Many different colours are used in the making of the
Lindisfarne Gospels. The common binding medium for the
colours was the white of egg, though perhaps a little fish
glue was also used. For some of the red the scribe used ker-
mes, obtained from insects living in the evergreen oaks of
the Mediterranean area. The indigo appears to have an ori-
ental origin, or it may be from woad belonging to northern

Europe. The pinks and purples come from a range of flowers and plants. The most exciting material for colouring is the lapis lazuli which makes the blue, for it seems to have come from Badakshan in the foothills of the Himalayas. This makes us realize that, being in the sea, the Island was on the main trading routes of its day, and not as remote as some like to imagine. Did the scribe purposely collect his colours from all the known world to show how the Gospels are for the whole world?

I like the words of Geraldus of Wales concerning another great manuscript which he saw in the twelfth century; they are meant to make you stop and wonder:

> *If you take the trouble to look very closely, and penetrate with your eyes the secrets of the artistry you will notice such intricacies, so delicate and subtle, so close together and well knitted, so involved and bound together, and so fresh still in their colourings, that you will not hesitate to declare that all these things must have been the result of the work, not of men, but of angels.*[9]

It is believed that all of the artwork and the actual script was done by one man and that it took him about two years. There is a note at the end of the Lindisfarne Gospels which tells us of its writer, its binder, who decorated it and by whom the note was written. Although it was written by Aldred at Chester-le-Street in County Durham over 250 years after the Gospels were crafted there is no need to doubt its accuracy.

> *Eadfrith, Bishop of Lindisfarne, originally wrote this book, for God and for Saint Cuthbert and, jointly, for the saints whose relics are on this island. Ethelwald, Bishop of Lindisfarne islanders, impressed it on the outside and covered it, as he well knew how to do. And Billfrith, the hermit, forged the ornaments which are on it on the outside, and adorned it with gold and*

with gems and also with silver-gilt – pure metal. And Aldred, unworthy and most miserable priest, glossed it in English between the lines with the help of God and Saint Cuthbert.

So the actual crafting of this wonderful book is down to Eadfrith who became Bishop of Lindisfarne in May 689, a few months after the elevation of Cuthbert's body. It is almost certain that he completed the Gospels before he became bishop and before the elevation. Nothing is known about Eadfrith until after 689 except that he was a member of the monastery on Lindisfarne. Both *Lives* of Cuthbert, the anonymous *Life* by one of the monks of Lindisfarne, and Bede's *Life of Cuthbert* are dedicated to Eadfrith. We know that he also restored the hermitage on Inner Farne for Felgid, Cuthbert's second successor there. It was the two years of Eadfrith's life spent in the scriptorium on Lindisfarne that have left us one of the most wonderful books in the world. It is also interesting to note that he is the first English artist we know by name.

In the south aisle of the church there is a photo facsimile copy of the Lindisfarne Gospels in a glass case. This was presented to the church by Rockford College, Illinois, in 1970. The original is in the British Library and is on permanent display.

Give thanks to God for the Gospels and all who have handed them down to us.

> For Matthew and the birth stories of Jesus,
> *Glory and thanks to you, O Lord.*
> For Mark and the making of a faithful record,
> *Glory and thanks to you, O Lord.*
> For Luke and the healing miracles,
> *Glory and thanks to you, O Lord.*
> For John and the risen, mystical Christ,
> *Glory and thanks to you, O Lord.*
> For all who have preached the word,
> *Glory and thanks to you, O Lord.*
> For Eadfrith, Ethelwald and Billfrith,
> *Glory and thanks to you, O Lord.*
> For all who have followed the Scriptures,
> *Glory and thanks to you, O Lord.*
> For all translators and interpreters,
> *Glory and thanks to you, O Lord.*
> For the Word made flesh and dwelling among us,
> *Glory and thanks to you, O Lord.*

> *Blessed Lord,*
> *who caused all holy Scriptures to be written for our learning:*
> *help us so to hear them,*
> *to read, mark, learn and inwardly digest them*
> *that, through patience, and the comfort of your holy word,*
> *we may embrace and for ever hold fast the hope of everlasting life,*
> *which you have given us in our Saviour Jesus Christ.*
> *[ASB Collect for Advent II]*

8

Cuthbert's Island

To the west of the church is a grass-covered basaltic rock which is only accessible at low tide. If you turn right out of the church, go out of the small gate and then go left, it will lead you to where you can see this little island. This is 'Hobthrush' or 'St Cuthbert's Island'. This tiny island is less than a quarter of an acre in extent and is cut off from Holy Island by the tide in the same way that Holy Island is cut off from the mainland. The tide can come in very quickly here so you do need to be aware of the state of the tide. In the late spring this small island has a good covering of sea pinks and campion. From this island, in the summer, it is possible to hear the singing of the seals and watch the sun set directly behind Cheviot. In winter, when the tide comes in, the island is a haven for the waders, oystercatchers and eider duck.

The wooden cross was erected in the 1930s as a memorial to two lads lost at sea. Below the cross are traces of a

medieval chapel which was known as St Cuthbert's in the Sea. This little chapel is about 13 feet wide and 25 feet long. The chapel is surrounded by a wall that could be a vallum, like the one around the monastery, marking out the sacred space. Some think it is only a breakwater, but this is unlikely. Bede describes St Cuthbert's Island as being 'in the outer precincts of the monastery', so the wall here could at least be a symbolic and ritual extension of the monastic vallum. It is possible that this medieval chapel has obliterated any remains from the time of Aidan and Cuthbert. To the north of the chapel is a low mound which could be the remains of a small beehive cell of the type common to the Celts of Ireland. If this is so, it could be the very cell that Aidan or Cuthbert used. More research needs to be done on this island.

Along the small beach on Holy Island in front of this island can be found 'Saint Cuthbert's beads'. These beads are in reality the fossilized remains of a sea creature called a 'crinoid', a lily-shaped creature of the Echinodermata family – the family that includes starfish and sea urchins. The crinoid was anchored to the sea by a stalk up to three feet long. The animal on top of the stem was star-shaped like the calyx of a sea lily. When the animal died the stalk sank to the sea bed and so became fossilized. Usually the discs of the stalk all broke up and these discs form the beads we call 'Cuthbert's beads'. If the tide prevents you from going to Cuthbert's Island you can at least look along this little beach for Cuthbert's Beads. If the tide is in you are also more likely to see the eider duck on the edge of Cuthbert's Island. The male duck is black and white and the female rich brown.

In *Marmion* Sir Walter Scott tells the legend of Cuthbert's Beads:

> *... on a rock by Lindisfarne,*
> *Saint Cuthbert sits, and toils to frame*
> *The sea-borne beads that bear his name:*

Such tales had Whitby fishers told;
And said they might his shape behold,
And hear his anvil sound:
A deaden'd clang – a huge dim form,
Seen but, and heard, when gathering storm
And night were closing round.

[Marmion 2.16]

Cuthbert, like Aidan before him and others after him, used this island as a hermitage. Bede says: 'At the beginning of his solitary life, he retired to a certain place in the outer precincts of the monastery which seemed more secluded.' But the island was too accessible, so another place was sought for his spiritual combat. Bede says: 'When he had fought there in solitude for some time with the invisible enemy, by prayer and fasting, he sought a place of combat farther and more remote from mankind, aiming at greater things.' Here Bede is talking of the Inner Farne Island.

Later still, when Cuthbert's body was being disinterred in the Lent of 698, Edbert, the Bishop of Lindisfarne, was on St Cuthbert's Island. Bede tells us: 'At that time he was living alone at some distance from the church in a place surrounded by the sea, where he used always to spend Lent and the forty days before the Nativity of our Lord in fasting, prayer and penitence.'[10] It would seem that there was a tradition of the leaders of the church on Lindisfarne to use Cuthbert's Island as their place of retreat, where they could get away from the rest of the monastery.

Once again here is a visual image that reminds us of the need of a balanced life: we all need our times of openness and accepting what comes to us, but also our times of retreat and silence when we can be still before our God. Pray that we may learn the rhythm of the tides, of ebbing and flowing, of action and stillness. Think upon this:

Do you ever feel you have spent all your energy, all your life, for nothing?

Perhaps the light has gone out of your life and you are in the dark.

It is as if some great ebb-tide has come upon you.

In its going out it has taken all away and left you quite bare.

So it was with the disciples, they had toiled all night and gained nothing.

We know from experience that they had lost more than they had gained.

There is a strange feeling that they have been here before.

I have been there many times, I know the ebb tide.

Then the light dawns on a new day, new opportunities, new hopes – if we can rise to it.

There is a brightness seeking to enter our lives.

Will we cling to the shadows? Are we determined to stay in the dark?

It is then He comes – the tide turns, what was on ebb begins to flow.

He is there waiting for us.

Perhaps we had to be emptied to make room for Him.

Perhaps we had to make retreat so that He could advance towards us.

'When morning came Jesus stood on the shore.'

Here on this little beach, in front of Cuthbert's Island, in the dark, we light our Easter Fire.

Light triumphs over darkness,

Life triumphs over death,

Love triumphs over hatred.

We have the victory through Him who loves us.

Alleluia.

I often see Cuthbert's Island in the mist. Sometimes I am in the fog myself, then I pray a prayer from the Hebridean Islands:

> Though the dawn breaks cheerless on this isle today,
> My spirit walks in a path of light.
> For I know my greatness, Thou hast built me a throne within thy heart.
> I dwell safely within the circle of Thy care.
> I cannot fall for a moment out of Thine everlasting arms.
> I am on my way to Thy glory.

[Alistair Maclean, *Hebridean Altars*][11]

9

The Battle Stone

In the English Heritage museum there is a wonderful stone depicting some warriors. On one side of the stone is a group of warriors hastening to battle, on the other side a cross with hands each side of it and the sun and moon above it. The stone is obviously from around the eighth to ninth centuries. There has been much speculation about what it commemorates. The design looks more Pictish than anything else on the Island. The most popular theory is that it is about the Viking invasion in 793. On one side are the Viking warriors and on the other the symbols of Christ.

This was certainly a battle that was remembered. In a letter addressed to King Aethelred of Northumbria, Alcuin writes of the invasion: 'Behold, the church of St Cuthbert

spattered with the blood of the priests of God, despoiled of all its ornaments, a place more venerable than all in Britain is given as prey to pagan peoples'.[12] In another letter, addressed to the Bishop of Lindisfarne, Alcuin writes: 'The calamity of your situation saddens me every day, though I am absent. When the pagans desecrated the sanctuaries of God, and poured out the blood of the saints around the altar, laid waste the house of our hope, trampled on the bodies of the saints in the Temple of God.'[13]

The Anglo-Saxon Chronicle for the same year, 793, is very dramatic:

> *In this year fierce, foreboding omens came over the land of Northumbria and wretchedly terrified the people. There were excessive whirlwinds, lightning storms, and fiery dragons were seen flying in the sky. These signs were followed by a great famine, and shortly after in the same year the ravaging of heathen men destroyed God's church at Lindisfarne through brutal robbery and slaughter.'* [14]

Look at the Battle Stone and remember the Viking invasion. But I am not convinced, for there are very few memorials set up by the losers of battles. I wonder if it could be about the battle of Heavenfield? On one side are Oswald's warriors going out to defeat a far greater army: it would take a miracle to bring about a victory. Yet Oswald did win, and so invited the Irish monks of Iona to come as missionaries into Northumbria. Before the battle of Heavenfield Oswald raised up a cross and held it with his own hands – hands that were later said to be imperishable. The battle took place before the day dawned, perhaps the reason for the sun and the moon. The stone could well commemorate the battle that made the foundation of Holy Island possible.

It is good to reflect on these two battles. Oswald's was a great victory, whereas the Viking invasions led to destruction. Life is often a battle, we all have struggles to survive. Do we know how to lift up the cross like Oswald? Do we find hope and strength in our God?

A third idea is that the stone is not about an earthly battle at all: it is about the Day of Judgement. In the time of the Irish and Saxon monks on Lindisfarne, the Day of Judgement, the time of the last great battle, was very much a strong part of their faith and teaching. Look again on the cross side and know who wins the battle, the Christ who triumphs. Know that in Him we are more than conquerors. Know that, no matter how fierce the battle, He has promised we 'shall not perish but have everlasting life'. Give thanks that in Him we are more than conquerors:

> *Lord you have triumphed over evil,*
> *Good Lord deliver us.*
> *You have defeated the powers of darkness,*
> *Good Lord deliver us.*
> *You have won victory over the grave,*
> *Good Lord deliver us.*
> *You bring strength to our weakness,*
> *Good Lord deliver us.*
> *You bring hope to our blindness,*
> *Good Lord deliver us.*
> *You bring joy to our sadness,*
> *Good Lord deliver us.*
> *From all that would defeat us,*
> *Good Lord deliver us.*

> *Lord grant us peace,*
> *Peace in our hearts, peace in our minds,*
> *Peace in our homes, peace in our work,*
> *Peace in our relationships, peace in our dealings,*
> *Peace in our community, peace in our world.*
> *The deep, deep peace of God be upon us and all creation.*

10

The Priory

To enter the Priory tickets need to be obtained from the English Heritage museum.

The early Celtic monastery was of wooden buildings and wattle and daub. The church was of oak and thatched. After 664 and the Synod of Whitby the buildings would become grander, but there are no Saxon remains of any note apart from the pillow stones in the Priory museum and the Saxon stonework in the Parish Church. So nothing remains of the early Priory, we are not even sure of its site though we can guess the shape of its enclosure. As you would expect, most of the buildings would be relatively near the church or churches.

In 875 the monks left Lindisfarne. Simeon of Durham, describing the Cuthbert Congregation, says, 'They wandered throughout the whole district of Northumbria, having no settled dwelling place; they were like sheep flying before wolves.' On their departure it is not known if the Island was left totally uninhabited, but if it was it would not be for long. With plenty of fish and shellfish and good land, it would not be left untended. Yet for more than two centuries we know little of what happened on the Island.

In 1069 the last Saxon bishop, Ethelwine, came back to Lindisfarne for the winter, with Cuthbert's body and other relics, fearing William the Conqueror and his harrying of the north. They were all returned to Durham in spring 1070. This was the last time the Lindisfarne Gospels were on the Island. In 1082 the Cuthbert Congregation at Durham was replaced by Benedictine monks. William of Calais, the Bishop of Durham, gave the church at Lindisfarne to the Benedictines. Within two years the Island became known as 'Holy Island'. From then on Holy Island remained in a subordinate position as a Priory belonging to Durham; the Mother Church had become the daughter.

Building began on the Island, the new Priory Church being started in 1093. An ancient account says that a monk called Edward built the Priory in honour of St Cuthbert. The stone for the building came from the mainland. People from the district around helped in carting the stone, providing the transport and the labour. The Priory Church dedicated to St Peter was completed in the first half of the twelfth century. During this time it is more than likely that the Parish Church was used as the main place of worship.

In the Priory there would only be about five to six Benedictines to maintain the daily services and care for the pilgrims and islanders. The endowments of the parish which brought in the income were the Island, the manors of Fenham and Shoreswood, plus various farms on the mainland. The caring for the Priory and the running of the estate would occupy all the time of these monks.

Under the Benedictines the Island would have a settled way of life and a steady stream of pilgrims for four and a half centuries. The monks from Durham were not all that keen on serving on Holy Island, as the way of life was much harder on the Island than at the Mother House. Though the Island was not raided, its lands on the mainland suffered from the Scots. The accounts for 1387–8 record: 'Tweedmouth, Ord, Murton, Scremerston, Cheswick, Goswick, Beil and Kilay, waste.' The next year was no better. The records say: 'Received from the farm of William de Bradfield twenty-six shillings and eight pence and no more, as it has been laid waste by our enemies the Scots ... No hay tithes received this year as they are all waste.'

This of course meant the monks were often quite hard up and found it difficult to maintain their work and buildings. If it had not been for the generosity of the Earl of Northumberland, when the whole land was laid waste in 1384 the

Priory would have been desperate indeed. So life for the monks, though not dangerous, was often extremely hard.

The main west doorway of the Priory Church was completed by around 1150 and intended only for special services and ceremonial occasions. The normal entry to the Priory would be by the main gate in the outer court. Now you enter directly into the Priory Church through the west door. Do remember it is still a church even if without a roof, and down in the present chancel lay Cuthbert and the relics of many saints. Many groups of pilgrims still use this church for their worship throughout the summer. Pause and give thanks to God for the holy men who served him here.

Many of the characteristics of the church are copied from Durham Cathedral and are in the Norman style. The original chancel, which was small and had an apse, was extended in the thirteenth century. The building had three towers, two at the west doorway and a central tower over the transept crossing. One of the two ribs which supported the central tower still stands and is known by all as the 'Rainbow Arch'.

The pillars on the north side have zig-zag and diaper fluting like that at Durham. It was after the battle of Bannockburn that Northumberland was repeatedly raided by the Scots. Along with many other northern monasteries Holy Island was fortified. Traces of these fortifications can be seen along the walls of the outer court with its parapet, walk and battlements.

The dissolution of the monasteries, under Henry VIII in 1537, brought about a new chapter for the Priory. The fifty-ninth, and last, Prior of Lindisfarne, Thomas Sparke, was pensioned off as Suffragan Bishop of Berwick. The Priory was soon being employed as 'the Queen Majestie's storehouse'. In 1543 an army was assembled within the Priory to repel any Scottish invasion. Soon stone was being taken away from the Priory to help to build the Castle on Beblowe Crag. In the year 1613 Lord Walden, Earl of Dunbar, despoiled the Priory by taking the lead off the roof, the bells and anything else of value. His heavily laden ship sailed out of the harbour and soon afterwards sank in a storm. Local fishermen say they think they know where the lead lies on the sea bed. Once opened to the elements the Priory went into decay. When stone was needed for building or repair the Priory was plundered.

Think upon this holy site: here the bones of Aidan and Cuthbert were buried, here the early saints worshipped. Here in the Norman Priory about five monks led their disciplined lives and regularly maintained the monastic services throughout each day.

Come Lord discipline us
That we may be your disciples.
Come into our time
and fill it with eternity.
Come Lord discipline us.
Come into our work
and fill it with glory.
Come Lord discipline us.
Come into our communities
and fill them with peace.
Come Lord discipline us.
Come into our churches
and fill them with love.
Come Lord discipline us.
Come into our days
and fill them with light.
Come Lord discipline us
That we may be your disciples.

Father, we give you thanks for the faithful who have maintained
worship in this place.
With the countless peoples who have sung your praises:
With the faithful witnesses to your Word:
With the ministers of sacraments and loving pastors:
With the worshippers who live here and the holy pilgrims:
With the church on earth, one with the church in heaven:
We seek to join our praises, in the name of Christ our Lord.

11

The Heugh

The Heugh is the only real hill on Holy Island, apart from the 100-foot Beblowe Crag on which the Castle stands. The Heugh is easily approachable from the south-east corner of the market place. You go through Sanctuary Close and get an excellent view of the little harbour and its upturned boats. Go and stand on the Heugh. It is only sixty-two feet high; some of the sand dunes are higher at over seventy feet. Yet from here is one of the most magnificent views in the whole of the British Isles. Southwards, just over the water by the two tall navigation beacons, is where Urien ap Rheged met his end. This Celtic defeat helped to make the history of England and make us the land of the 'English'. Here in this peaceful spot was the last organized stand of the British in the north. Somewhere out there Urien's headless body lies buried in an oak coffin.

Further south is Bamburgh Castle standing proudly above all. It was on this site that Edwin had his fortress and St Paulinus came as a missionary from Rome. From the same place Oswald sent to Iona for missionaries and Aidan came in response. One Easter in this fortress Oswald gave to the poor not only the food from his table but the silver plates the food was on. It was this fortress that was attacked by Penda, the pagan king of Mercia, who, in the seventh century, was such a threat to Northumbria and to Christianity. He tried to set the Castle alight. Bede tells us Aidan was on Inner Farne, saw what was happening and prayed to God. The wind direction changed and the fire did not destroy the Castle. Penda left without victory.

Looking to the right of the Castle you can pick out the village of Bamburgh and the church tower. It was whilst visiting a church on this site that Aidan died. In the present

51

church is a part of the beam he lay against when he died. This beam has survived at least two fires. In Bamburgh churchyard Grace Darling is buried, and there is a little museum dedicated to her opposite the church.

If you turn northwards and look slightly to the west you will see the Lammermuir hills. It was here, on the night that Aidan died, that Cuthbert had a vision. Now still looking northwards but along the coast line you can see a range of cliffs in the distance: on a clear day you may be able to pick out the lighthouse. This is St Abb's Head. Here the sister of Oswald, Ebba, had a monastery for men and women. It was at the foot of the cliffs at St Abb's that Cuthbert spent the night praying in the sea and when he came out of the water early in the morning two otters were seen playing around his feet and drying them with their fur.

Turn now and look eastwards. Out at sea there is a chain of islands well strung out: this is the Farne Islands. This group of about twenty-five islands is the most easterly end of the Great Whin Sill. The northerly island with the lighthouse is Longstone. It was from Longstone that Grace Darling and her father rowed out in tumultuous seas to rescue the ship-wrecked from the Forfarshire.

The island nearest to Bamburgh is Inner Farne which has been used as a retreat and hermitage by so many holy men. At low tide Inner Farne boasts about sixteen acres, mostly bare rock: at best there are about five acres of thin peaty soil. The whole island is covered by sea spray in any gale. Yet it teems with bird life. Terns dive and dart at visitors in the nesting season. Puffins in their thousands dodge the gulls to bring in sand eels to their young in the burrows. Shags, cormorants, razorbills and guillemots colonize the cliffs. The sound of the kittiwake is always heard. The eider duck finds its home and protection here. Seals are all around these islands.

The first person we know to use Inner Farne as a hermitage was Aidan, though Cuthbert is the one of whom many stories are told. Today the Inner Farne is managed by the National Trust and is a bird sanctuary. For a good part of the year boat trips are possible to the Farnes from North Sunderland. It was on Inner Farne that Cuthbert died on 29th March 687. The night he died a signal of a bonfire was lit to tell a watcher, standing on the Heugh on Holy Island, that the holy Cuthbert had died. No doubt monks stood on the Heugh to watch Cuthbert's body be brought back by sea to Lindisfarne.

West from the Heugh Cuthbert's Island lies below you. Here better than anywhere you can see the tide come around this little piece of land. Look across to the mainland and the Kyloe Hills which have a cave on their western side called 'Cuthbert's Cave'. Beyond these hills lies the highest hill on the eastern side of England – the Cheviot. The Cheviot hill country is where Aidan, and later Cuthbert, often went to meet people in their villages.

On the Heugh itself, not far from the war memorial designed by Lutyens, there are signs of very ancient buildings. It is thought that from the time of the Celtic monastery there were buildings on this hill. There is a little squared mound near the war memorial that is thought to be the base of a building, perhaps a watch tower. It was from such a watch tower that a monk was stationed to watch Inner Farne for news of Cuthbert. From the Heugh local fishermen – and their wives – have anxiously looked out when a boat has been delayed. The little roofless building to the west of the Lookout is know as the 'shippel' – it may have been a chapel. Here people would shelter as they sought the seas for signs of returning boats.

From the Heugh there is an excellent view of the Parish Church, the Priory and the Castle. The whole panoramic view contains so much of the history of our land. Here in microcosm is the story of our nation; we should stop awhile and take it all in.

Father, we thank you for the lives of the saints.
God of Aidan the gentle one,
You are with us now.
God of Oswald the generous one,
You are with us now.
God of Finan the missionary one,
You are with us now.
God of Colman the steadfast one,
You are with us now.
God of Cedd the preaching one,
You are with us now.
God of Chad the humble one,
You are with us now.
God of Cuthbert the holy one,
You are with us now.
God of Eadfrith the artistic one,
You are with us now.
Amen. Alleluia.

The God of goodness, the God of grace, the God of glory,
The Lord of light, the Lord of love, the Lord of life,
The Spirit of power, the Spirit of peace, the Spirit of praise,
Be with us in our journey, in our homes, now and evermore.

References

1 From the Venerable Bede, *The History of the English Church and People* ed. Leo Price (Penguin, 1955)

2 From *A Welsh Pilgrim's Manual* ed. Brendan O'Malley (Gomer Press, 1989)

3 The Venerable Bede op. cit.

4 The Venerable Bede op. cit.

5 From Bertram Colgrave, *Two Lives of St Cuthbert* (Cambridge University Press, 1985)

6 From *Two Lives of St Cuthbert* op. cit.

7 From *Two Lives of St Cuthbert* op. cit.

8 From the *Exeter Book,* a tenth-century volume kept in the Library of Exeter Cathedral

9 From Susan Youngs ed., *The Work of Angels* (British Museums Publications, 1989)

10 Quotations from *Two Lives of St Cuthbert* op. cit.

11 Alistair Maclean, *Hebridean Altars* (Moray Press, Edinburgh and London, 1937)

12 Quoted in Magnus Magnusson, *Lindisfarne* (Oriel Press, 1984)

13 Quoted in John Marsden, *The Fury of the Northmen* (Book Club Associates, 1993)

14 From Anne Savage ed., *The Anglo-Saxon Chronicles* (Book Club Associates, 1983)